POSTERS AND PROPAGANDA
IN WARTIME

WEAPONS OF MASS PERSUASION

DANIEL JAMES AND RUTH THOMSON

W
FRANKLIN WATTS
LONDON•SYDNEY

IN ASSOCIATION WITH

IMPERIAL WAR MUSEUM

First published in 2007 by Franklin Watts

Copyright © 2007 Franklin Watts

Franklin Watts
338 Euston Road
London NW1 3BH

Franklin Watts Australia
Level 17/207 Kent Street
Sydney, NSW 2000

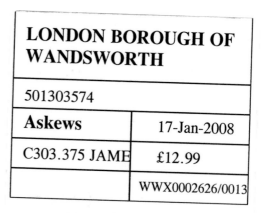

A CIP catalogue record for this book is available from the British Library.

Dewey number: 769'.499403

ISBN: 978 0 7496 7117 4

Printed in China

Franklin Watts is a division of Hachette Children's Books, an Hachette Livre UK company.

Designer: Jason Billin
Editor: Sarah Ridley
Art Director: Jonathan Hair
Editor in Chief: John C. Miles

Picture credits
Front cover left, from top: PST 2734 © IWM, PST 11408 © IWM, PST 10304 © IWM, PST 2916 IWM repro right.
bottom row, from left: PST 2871 IWM repro right, PST 000192 IWM repro right, PST 003158 IWM repro right,
PST 2832 IWM repro right.

Back cover, right, from top: PST 2763 © IWM, PST 0311 © IWM, PST 003645 IWM repro right,
PST 14971 IWM repro right, PST 6229 IWM repro right.

Insides: p4 t Popperfoto, 4m Popperfoto, 4b PST 11499 © IWM; p5 from top: PST 11391 © IWM, PST 00402 ©IWM,
PST 10165 © IWM, PST 13387 © IWM, PST 12182 © IWM; p6 PST 002734 © IWM; p7 PST 0321 © IWM; p8 from left:
PST 5069 © IWM, PST 11391 © IWM, PST 0566 © IWM, PST 4903 © IWM; p9 PST 11499 © IWM; p10 t PST 11408 ©
IWM, 10 b PST 5119 © IWM; p11 PST 0566 © IWM; p12t PST 4903 © IWM, 12b PST 2763 © IWM, p13 PST 5162 ©
IWM; p14t PST 0314 © IWM, 14b PST 000311 © IWM; 15 PST 5030 © IWM; p16l PST 13172 © IWM, p16r PST 000402
© IWM; p17 PST 7813 © IWM; p18l PST 10063 © IWM, 18r PST 10179 © IWM; p19 PST 10304 © IWM; p20 PST 6543
© IWM; p21 from top: PST 000145 IWM repro right, PST 3673 IWM repro right, PST 003642 IWM repro right;
PST 3108 IWM repro right; p22 PST 00136 IWM repro right; p23t PST 000071 IWM repro right, p23b PST 0096 IWM
repro right; p24t PST 000076 IWM repro right, 24b PST 003095 IWM repro right; p25 PST 000135 IWM repro right;
p26l PST 0059 IWM repro right; p26r PST 2916 IWM repro right; p27t PST 008105 IWM repro right; p27b PST 6080
IWM repro right; p28t PST 002817 IWM repro right, p28b PST 003750 IWM repro right; p29 PST 2871 IWM repro
right; p30 PST 2832 IWM repro right; p31t PST 8286 IWM repro right, p30b PST 2831 IWM repro right; p32t PST 6229
IWM repro right, p32b Popperfoto; p33 PST 13888 IWM repro right; p34 PST 003645 IWM repro right; p35 PST
000192 IWM repro right; p36t PST 14971 IWM repro right, p36b PST 14972 IWM repro right; p37t PST 14886 IWM
repro right, p37b PST 002911 IWM repro right; p38l PST 003158 IWM repro right, p38r PST 8250 IWM repro right;
p39 PST 0010 IWM repro right; p40 PST 3108 IWM repro right; p41t PST 14961 IWM repro right, p41b PST 3406 IWM
repro right; p42 PST 14752 IWM repro right; p43t PST 14775 IWM repro right, p43b PST 000705 IWM repro right; p44
Private Collection, Peter Newark Historical Pictures/Bridgeman Art Library; p45 PST 0176 IWM repro right; p46 PST
3107 IWM repro right; p47t PST 3929 © IWM, p47ml PST 003750 IWM repro right, p47mr from centre PST 2832,
2886, 2944 all IWM repro right; p47b PST 003642 IWM repro right.

The quotations used in this book are taken from Forgotten Voices of the Great War *and* Forgotten Voices of the Second
World War *by Max Arthur, copyright © Max Arthur and the Imperial War Museum, 2002.*

Contents

Introduction

During the First and Second World Wars, the British government produced millions of posters as part of its propaganda campaign.

Why posters?

Posters were cheap, quick and easy to produce. They could be put up almost anywhere and could contain varying mixtures of information and emotion. All of these factors made them ideal as weapons of mass persuasion.

Troops in a trench during the First World War.

What is propaganda?

Propaganda is a message that is designed to influence the beliefs or behaviour of a group of people. It can take many forms, but posters were the weapon of choice in both wars since other forms of mass communication were still limited.

Uses of posters

Posters had four main uses during wartime: to recruit an army, to increase the efficiency of the economy, to raise money and to boost morale. They also reminded people of their obligations and warned of dangers.

London ablaze, 1940.

Poster design

Posters had only a few seconds to do their job. As designers came to understand this better, messages were shortened to just a few words and an image was used to catch the eye and get the message across quickly.

How to read a poster

All the posters in this book were made for a reason. Try to work out what that reason is and whether the designer is being open about it or trying to hide it from you. Notice how the poster makes you feel and the tone of its text. Then think about the different techniques you might use to get your own way and see whether the same techniques are used in the poster. Watch out – the most persuasive posters make you absorb the message without even realising it.

First World War posters

Over 400 posters were issued in Britain from 1914 to 1918, with the following aims:

Recruitment

At the outbreak of war, the immediate priority for Britain was to create a 'mass army' to rival Germany. In the first sixteen months of the war, 2.5 million men joined up. However as the horrors of war became more apparent, recruitment dropped away, and posters had to become more ingenious in their methods of persuasion. By January 1916, when conscription was introduced, the Parliamentary Recruitment Committee had issued its 164th design of recruitment poster.

Women to work

As men left Britain to fight, there was a shortage of workers at home. The Ministry of Munitions, founded in 1915, was the first to issue a series of posters encouraging women to work. Many worked in factories and on the land. Others carried out support roles for the armed forces.

War bonds

The war was expensive, costing £1 million per day right from the start. By July 1915, the cost of the war had escalated so much that the Parliamentary War Savings Committee began a poster campaign urging people to buy war bonds. These raised funds for the war and reduced people's purchasing power, helping to keep the economy ticking over.

Save it

On 4 February 1915, the German government announced that the seas around Britain were to be considered a war zone and any Allied or neutral ship passing through them was liable to be sunk without warning. Poster campaigns encouraged people to save their food and coal to reduce the threat of mass starvation.

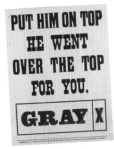

The end of the war

When the war had ended, posters soon turned their attention to domestic issues, such as the upcoming general election. By this stage people had become accustomed to a certain amount of wit and word-play in their posters, even when these concerned politics.

Man to man

In August 1914, at the outbreak of the war, Lord Kitchener was appointed war minister. His most pressing job was to increase army manpower as quickly as possible. His image was adopted by the Parliamentary Recruiting Committee (PRC), responsible for the majority of recruitment posters, and became one of the most iconic images of all time.

◄ Kitchener's authoritative image, with his unnerving stare, huge pointing finger and unforgettable moustache, gives this poster a powerful sense of personal appeal. It summarises the message you would get from a recruiting officer.

Why join up?

It was seeing the picture of Kitchener and his finger pointing at you – any position that you took up, the finger was always pointing at you.

Private Thomas McIndoe

► In contrast to the stern, imperative demand from Kitchener, other posters used appealing images of life as a soldier, such as this smiling example, to persuade men to join up.

ENLIST TO-DAY.

HE'S
HAPPY &
SATISFIED
—
ARE YOU ?

PUBLISHED BY THE PARLIAMENTARY RECRUITING COMMITTEE, LONDON. POSTER No 96.

PRINTED BY TURNER & DUNNETT, LONDON & LIVERPOOL.

For King and country

Many early posters appealed to a sense of patriotism, asking men explicitly to fight for their King, for their country or for their flag. Other posters used the emotive colours of the Union Flag – red, white and blue – to appeal to patriotic sentiment in a less explicit way.

▲ Patriotic images and colours catch the eye, even from a distance.

◀ Posters often depicted a Union Flag as a symbol of patriotism.

How did you join up?

I was astonished because I'd told him I was only seventeen and there I was, almost in the army. I went to the recruiting office and the officer said something to me about King and country and then he said, "Well raise your right hand and say I will," or something like that . . . to my amazement I found I was being called Private S C Lang.

Private S C Lang

▶ When the government needed to give complex information, such as how to enlist and who was affected by new conscription laws, text posters were used. This poster works as a 'proclamation' in an era without television and radio.

MORE MEN
ARE WANTED FOR
HIS MAJESTY'S ARMY

WHO MAY ENLIST.

All men who are 5 ft. 3 ins. and over, medically fit, and between 19 and 38, and all old soldiers up to 45.

TERMS OF ENLISTMENT.

You may join for the period of the War only if you do not want to serve for the ordinary period of the regular soldier. Then, as soon as the War is over, you will be able to return to your ordinary employment.

PAY.

Ordinary Army Pay (the lowest rate of pay is 7s. a week, less 1½d. for Insurance). Food, Clothing, Lodging and Medical Attendance provided free.

SEPARATION ALLOWANCES.

During the War the State, by the payment of Separation Allowance, helps the soldier to maintain his wife (if married before enlistment), children or dependants. The following are the weekly rates for the wife and children of a private soldier, including the allotment usually required from his pay:—

	Government Separation Allowance.			Largest Allotment required from Soldier.			Weekly Income Secured to Family.	
	s.	d.		s.	d.		s.	d.
For Wife only	9	0	...	3	6	...	12	6
„ and 1 Child	11	6	...	3	6	...	15	0
„ and 2 Children	14	0	...	3	6	...	17	6
„ and 3 Children	16	6	...	3	6	...	20	0
„ and 4 Children	18	6	...	3	6	...	22	0

For each additional child an additional Separation Allowance of 2s. is issuable.
Families living at the time of enlistment in the London Postal area are allowed by the State 3s. 6d. a week extra as long as they continue to live there.

Fuller particulars as to Separation Allowance, and as to Allowances to the Dependants of Unmarried Soldiers, and to the Motherless Children of Soldiers, can be obtained at any Recruiting Office or Post Office.

PENSIONS for the DISABLED.

Men disabled on service will be entitled after discharge to benefits under the Insurance Act IN ADDITION TO the Pension given by the War Office for partial or total disablement.

PROVISION for WIDOWS and CHILDREN.

The widows and children of soldiers who die on active service will continue to receive their Separation Allowances for a period which will not in any case exceed 26 weeks, and afterwards they will receive, SUBJECT TO CERTAIN QUALIFICATIONS, pensions at various rates.

HOW TO ENLIST.

Go to the nearest Post Office or Labour Exchange. There you will get the address of the nearest Recruiting Office, where you can enlist.

MEN ARE WANTED — ENLIST NOW.

PUBLISHED BY THE PARLIAMENTARY RECRUITING COMMITTEE, 12, DOWNING STREET, S.W.   Poster No. 33.   H. W. & V. Ld.   W.10754. 1/15.

Just war

A relatively small number of posters drew attention to alleged German atrocities, inciting moral outrage and justifying Britain's part in the war. These posters focused on the victims of German aggression – in particular Belgium, invaded by Germany in October 1914; Scarborough, Whitby and Hartlepool, English coastal towns which were shelled by the Germans on 16 December 1914; the *Lusitania*, a luxury passenger ship which was sunk by a German U-boat on 7 May 1915; and North Sea fishermen captured by the Germans. The posters appealed to certain characteristics and values, that it was felt all Britons shared and were worth fighting for.

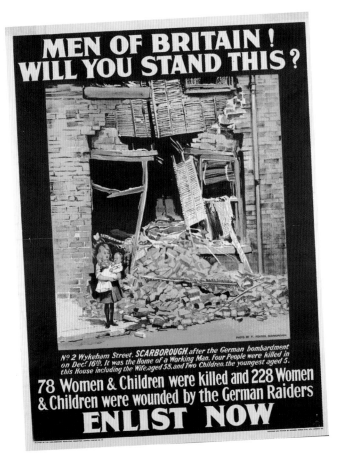

▲ This poster portrays a soldier neither in the heat of battle, nor even in the heat of emotion, but coolly standing firm. It appeals to the British sense of fair play, arguing that men must enlist in order to defend – and avenge – the victims of German aggression seen in the background.

◄ On the other hand, this poster preys on the fear of similar attacks taking place in the future. Although it overtly appeals to pride, its effect comes primarily from inciting fear that the recognisably British bricks may be the first of many to crumble unless more men enlist.

► Appealing to national pride, the colours of the Union Flag lend their authority to this call to arms.
The poster's tone might seem more apt if the subject were a playground squabble and not a world war.

THE KAISER'S INSULT

On August 19th, 1914, the Kaiser issued the following Order to his Army:

"It is my Royal and Imperial Command that you concentrate your energies, for the immediate present, upon one single purpose, and that is that you address all your skill and all the valour of my soldiers to exterminate first the treacherous English and walk over General French's contemptible little Army."

Fling the Kaiser's insult back in his teeth by making the "little" Army BIGGER— you can't make it BRAVER.

ENLIST NOW

PUBLISHED BY THE PARLIAMENTARY RECRUITING COMMITTEE, LONDON. Poster No. 6.   H. W. & V. Ld. W.6003, 10/14.

Women say GO!

TO THE
**YOUNG WOMEN
OF LONDON**

Is your "Best Boy" wearing Khaki? If not don't **YOU THINK** he should be?

If he does not think that you and your country are worth fighting for—do you think he is **WORTHY** of you?

Don't pity the girl who is alone—her young man is probably a soldier—fighting for her and her country—and for **YOU.**

If your young man neglects his duty to his King and Country, the time may come when he will **NEGLECT YOU.**

Think it over—then ask him to

JOIN THE ARMY TO-DAY

After the initial burst of direct and patriotic posters aimed at men, some posters produced in early 1915 adopted a more subtle approach – targeting men via the women in their lives. One poster even quoted Lady Macbeth, 'Stand not upon the order of your going, but go at once – enlist now!' These posters targeted girlfriends, wives and mothers with different emotional appeals to persuade their men to enlist.

◀ This text poster argues at length that women should be ashamed of a boyfriend who does not enlist. 'Wearing khaki' is a reference to soldiers' khaki uniforms.

A young man is given a white feather, a symbol of cowardice, by women

I was walking down the Camden High Street when two young ladies approached me and said, "Why aren't you in the Army with the boys?" So I said, "I'm sorry, but I'm only 17," and one of them said, "Oh, we've heard that one before. I suppose you're also doing work of national importance." Then she put her hand in her bag and pulled out a feather. I raised a hand thinking she was going to strike me and this feather was pushed right up my nose!

Private S C Lang

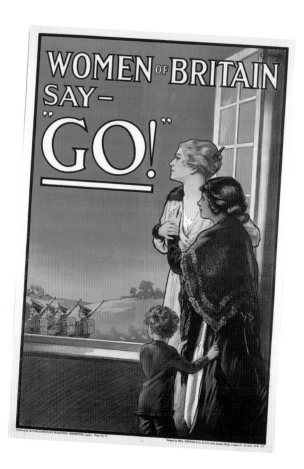

▲ As well as its direct message telling women to get their men to enlist, this poster also targets eligible men by showing vulnerable young women and children who need defending.

▲ This poster demonstrates the extent and scope of the recruitment campaign, as it tries to influence not only the young men eligible for enlistment but those around them. Here, their mothers are reminded that they should resist their maternal instinct to protect their sons and, instead, encourage their boys to do their duty to the country.

A mother's pride

When I enlisted in the ranks of the London Rifle Brigade, I found that my mother enjoyed a kind of spurious reflected glory. You see, she was in a local sewing shop, and of course everybody talked about their sons in the war, and my mother said, "Oh, Norman just enlisted," and this apparently created a great sensation...

Rifleman Norman Demuth

Shame

Another recruiting technique was to shame men into enlistment. Designers made men who had not enlisted feel as if they were failing to do their duty to King and country and this was something that they would later regret. Posters often showed a group of men who were all in it together, in contrast to the implied guilt of the viewer who had not joined up.

▶ The pointing figure of authority in this poster is John Bull, the traditional personification of Great Britain at the time. The implication is that even he would have enlisted by now.

Feelings of shame

The men in the line tended to despise conscientious objectors... I remember one man in particular who absolutely refused to have anything to do with the army at all... We took him to the open compound and as it was very cold at night we thought he'd be forced to wear khaki to keep himself warm, but he had other ideas. During the night he stripped himself of this khaki and shredded the whole of the suit up and hung it around the barbed wire and that man walked about all night without a shred of clothing on him. That was the type of treatment we had to mete out and I am utterly ashamed that I was forced to take part in it.

Sergeant C Lippett

▲ The designer Savile Lumley forces the viewer to imagine the shame of having to answer this question in post-war Britain. The poster was so emotionally manipulative that Lumley did not wish to be associated with it at the time.

Compulsion

During 1915 the number of men enlisting started to fall. British casualties from the beginning of the war to 9 October already numbered nearly 500,000. In addition, the supply of young, fit men was beginning to dry up. Many of the young men who had joined at the beginning of the war had joined for a lark thinking it would 'all be over by Christmas'. As it became clear that the war was going to last much longer, volunteers dwindled and more than half the men who were left were failing their medicals. Since the British Army badly needed more men, the government had no option but to take the unpopular move of introducing conscription.

◄ Even when it became compulsory to join up on 10 February 1916, posters were needed so that people knew that the law had changed. The act only applied to single men of military age, so posters like this offered single men one last chance to enlist voluntarily before being conscripted.

No surrender

We were not allowed to have white handkerchiefs in case we used them as a white flag.

Sergeant Thomas Painting

Calling all women!

As the army expanded rapidly, women were needed to take men's places on the land and in factories. The Ministry of Munitions, the Women's Land Army and Queen Mary's Army Auxiliary Corps all offered women the exciting prospect of a job previously reserved for men. They joined up in their thousands - by the end of the war, there were almost a million women working in munitions factories alone. Many men were concerned by the new earning power that women now had. To appease them, a special law was passed entitling men to reclaim their old jobs as soon as they returned from the front.

◀ The glorious sunset and the quotation set this poster in a religious context, appealing to a woman's sense of duty. The woman's anonymity makes her less engaging, but perhaps also less threatening to men who at the time were not used to women doing physical labour.

▶ Here the woman has been brought forward and she looks as though she has been interrupted getting ready for work. This is part of a different strategy – making the female viewer feel positive about her potential contribution, rather than focusing on her duty.

In 1916, a War Office investigation estimated that 12,000 men could be freed for the front line if women took over their non-combat roles. As a result, in February 1917, the Women's Army Auxiliary Corps (WAAC) started to recruit women. After performing exceptionally well, the WAAC was renamed Queen Mary's Army Auxiliary Corps with the then Queen as Commander-in-Chief on 9 April, 1918.

▲ The comic-book style and cheerful faces suggest safe adventures and camp-fire camaraderie. More than 25,000 women signed up to work as cooks, cleaners, clerks, ambulance drivers, telephonists, post-women and nurses.

Someone has to pay!

The war was hugely expensive, costing £1 million per day. By June 1915, £862 million had been spent on the war and urgent action had to be taken to raise more funds. In July 1915, the government started issuing war bonds. These were simply paper tokens – effectively an IOU from the government – promising to repay the amount they cost at a later date with added interest. The Parliamentary War Savings Committee (later the National War Savings Committee) issued almost 200 different posters aiming to raise funds in this way, making theirs the most extensive poster campaign of the First World War.

Local councils also used posters to advertise special fund-raising days that they put on for the National War Savings Committee. These days were usually themed around a new weapon, such as a tank or an aeroplane, but their goal was to sell war bonds.

▲ Designers thought of ways to show how the purchase of war bonds directly related to the outcome of the war.

▶ Aeroplane and tank weeks were held throughout the country in 1918. This poster asks people to spend money on the war by showing what their money would pay for – a high-tech weapon.

▶ This striking image from 1918, designed by Sidney Stanley, was first used with the text 'Feed the guns with war bonds'. It was re-worded to play to people's growing war-weariness.

BRING HIM HOME WITH WAR BONDS

SIDNEY STANLEY

Nº 128

Save, don't waste

Britain was reliant on imported food and supplies for its survival. Germany exploited this by using U-boats to sink Britain's merchant ships. By 1917, this was causing severe shortages for the British. Posters asked people to save wheat, use less coal and recycle whenever possible.

◀ This poster reminded viewers that saving food would not only prevent their own hunger, but also the danger that sailors endured to get food into Britain.

A Royal Marine talks about the end of the war

The Armistice came, the day we had dreamed of. The guns stopped, the fighting stopped... I should have been happy. I was sad. I thought of the slaughter, the hardships, the waste and the friends I had lost.

Sergeant-Major Richard Tobin

Second World War posters

When Britain declared war on Germany on 3 September 1939, measures for the conscription of males were already in place, so poster campaigns concentrated on other issues.

Public safety

The government issued important safety information in posters about gas masks, air-raid shelters, the blackout and evacuation. They also warned against the dangers of giving away secrets to enemy spies with careless talk.

Specialist recruitment

The government needed as many women as possible to join the auxiliary services to free up men for combat. To keep the economy running smoothly, the government also needed women to fill the jobs left behind by male conscripts. Not all recruitment campaigns, however, were targeted solely at women. Others encouraged both men and women to join the Auxiliary Fire Service (AFS) and men to volunteer for the Home Defence Battalions.

Raising morale

After France surrendered in June 1940, the threat of a German invasion from across the Channel was at its peak. The next couple of years were the hardest for Britain, so many posters were concerned with raising morale. They featured inspiring words from Winston Churchill, images of a Britain that was worth fighting for, or reassuring portrayals of Britain united with her allies and colonies.

Food and supplies

There were severe shortages of food, clothes and raw materials during the war. This was partly because British industry focused almost exclusively on the war effort. It was also because German U-boats almost severed Britain's supply lines by attacking merchant ships. The government responded to shortages with campaigns telling people to grow their own vegetables, reduce consumption of essentials, limit their spending on luxuries and start recycling.

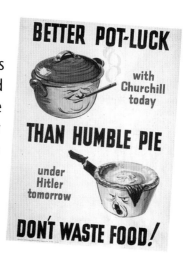

Watch out!

Air Raid Precautions (ARP) was a government organisation originally planned in 1924 to protect the country from aerial bombing. With war looming, the biggest immediate threat was thought to come from the German air force, the Luftwaffe. The ARP's responsibilities included distributing gas masks and home air-raid shelters, maintaining public air-raid shelters, enforcing the blackout and rescuing civilians after bombing raids. Posters were used to educate the public about new habits and new pieces of equipment that they would need to defend themselves against the Luftwaffe threat.

▶ In 1938, 38 million gas masks were issued to civilians. Posters told people how to use the new pieces of equipment. As it turned out, Hitler never ordered the use of gas against the British, but regular gas drills and posters like this kept the nation on the alert.

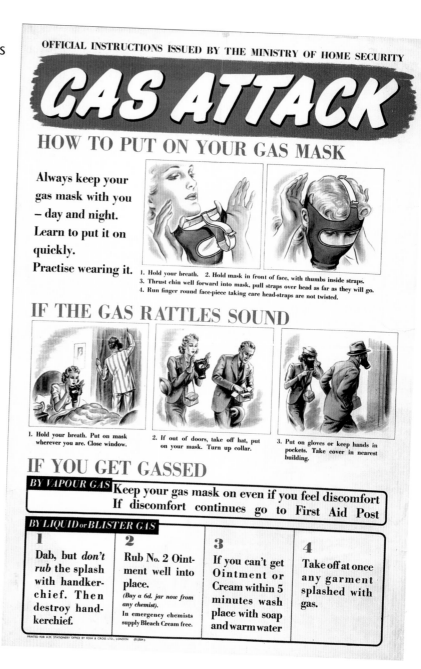

OFFICIAL INSTRUCTIONS ISSUED BY THE MINISTRY OF HOME SECURITY

GAS ATTACK

HOW TO PUT ON YOUR GAS MASK

Always keep your gas mask with you – day and night. Learn to put it on quickly. Practise wearing it.

1. Hold your breath. 2. Hold mask in front of face, with thumbs inside straps.
3. Thrust chin well forward into mask, pull straps over head as far as they will go.
4. Run finger round face-piece taking care head-straps are not twisted.

IF THE GAS RATTLES SOUND

1. Hold your breath. Put on mask wherever you are. Close window.

2. If out of doors, take off hat, put on your mask. Turn up collar.

3. Put on gloves or keep hands in pockets. Take cover in nearest building.

IF YOU GET GASSED

BY VAPOUR GAS Keep your gas mask on even if you feel discomfort
If discomfort continues go to First Aid Post

BY LIQUID or BLISTER GAS

1	2	3	4
Dab, but *don't rub* the splash with handkerchief. Then destroy handkerchief.	Rub No. 2 Ointment well into place. *(Buy a 6d. jar now from any chemist).* In emergency chemists supply Bleach Cream free.	If you can't get Ointment or Cream within 5 minutes wash place with soap and warm water	Take off at once any garment splashed with gas.

PRINTED FOR H.M. STATIONERY OFFICE BY FOSH & CROSS LTD., LONDON   (51/504.)

A false alarm

I thought it was awfully funny, although I suppose I shouldn't say that in a war – but when the warning went there was a chappie who lived at the end of the street. He was under the impression that as soon as the warning went he had to put his mask on. He did this over and over again, running through the street with it on. We had been told only to use the gas mask if we heard the rattles. And that the normal warning was for getting into your shelter.

Doris Scott

By the end of August 1939, 2 million steel shelters had already been made. There were two types of official domestic air-raid shelter – the outdoor Anderson shelter and the indoor Morrison shelter, which was introduced in 1941. The Morrison shelter, shown here, came in kit form and had to be put together at home.

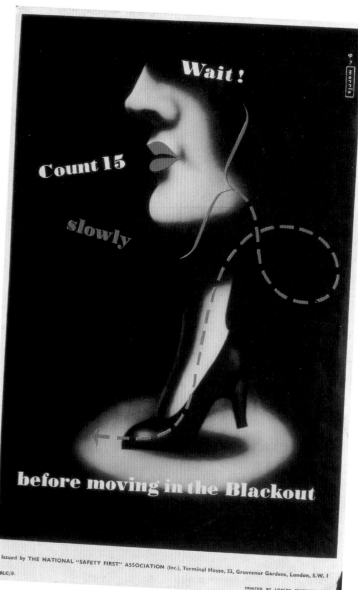

On 1 September the blackout began. Street and car lights were dimmed while windows and doors had to be covered with thick black material. The blackout may have helped prevent some German bombers from finding their targets but the number of people killed on the roads rose dramatically.

The King's Surgeon has a grumble about the blackout

Frightening the nation into blackout regulations, the Luftwaffe was able to kill 600 British citizens a month [through road traffic accidents] without ever taking to the air, at a cost to itself of exactly nothing.

Wilfred Trotter

Evacuate!

The government planned to evacuate city children to families in the countryside, where it was thought they would be safe from German bombs. The order was given on 31 August 1939 and the first major evacuation, Operation Pied Piper, began the next day.

▶ Between 1 and 3 September, 1.9 million mothers and children were successfully evacuated from London and the south-east. This poster tried to reassure mothers that their children would be safer away from London. It shows children sheltering in an urban setting.

MOTHERS Send them out of London

Give them a chance of greater safety and health

DON'T do it, mother –

LEAVE THE CHILDREN WHERE THEY ARE

ISSUED BY THE MINISTRY OF HEALTH

◀ At first, the expected air raids did not happen. Many mothers began to think their children would be better off at home and as many as 60 per cent of the evacuees returned before the Blitz began for real in September 1940. In this poster a ghostly Adolf Hitler, the Nazi dictator, tells a mother to return her children to the cities.

What was being evacuated like?

For children, it was extremely exciting. I don't think this has come over enough. It was a great adventure... But when it came to the moment when we lined up and your mum and dad were on one side of the road and you were on the other – then we all just burst into tears, the lot of us.

Ronald McGill

▼ When the Blitz did begin, one in ten British casualties were children as thousands of evacuees had returned home. This poster was produced towards the end of 1940. The fireman plays the role of a friendly but firm father figure both to the child and the viewer.

What was it like when the evacuees had left?

Mum said that after we left it was like a cathedral. It was so quiet, the whole area. In the evenings, she said, it was unbelievable. They didn't realise 'til then the noise of children playing. The streets had been our playground.

Ronald McGill

Dig for victory

Before the war, three-quarters of Britain's food was imported each year. After the war began, the government realised that reliance on imported food would have to be reduced. Further shortages meant that food rationing was introduced in January 1940. Later in the war the government produced posters encouraging everyone to run their own allotment. It invented the characters 'Dr Carrot' and 'Potato Pete' to help parents get young people eating food which could be grown easily at home.

▲ By the end of the war there were 1.7 million allotments, thanks in large part to the 'Dig for Victory' campaign which successfully dramatised the connection between growing vegetables and winning the war.

▲ Bold in style and reliant on a striking visual pun, this poster is typical of the artist Abram Games, whose maxim was 'maximum effect, minimum means'.

The carrot's reputation was boosted after it was claimed that carrots helped people see in the dark – very useful in the time of the blackout. British Intelligence spread the rumour that carrots were helping the RAF pilots to see and shoot down Luftwaffe planes in the dark, in order to hide their newly invented radar system from their German counterparts.

Oranges and lemons

My sister didn't know what a banana was until after the war and oranges were kept for pregnant women and small children under five.

Joan Reed

The production of potatoes tripled during the war. 'Potato Pete' even had his own popular song.

Who's listening?

The government was determined to learn from mistakes in the First World War, when valuable information about sailing times and troop movements had inadvertently been given away. From February 1940 onwards, the Ministry of Information distributed more than 2.5 million posters, with the theme 'Careless talk costs lives', to ports and transport centres, where discretion was particularly important, as well as to public meeting places such as pubs and offices.

◄ This poster gives a clear instruction to keep quiet, ('keep mum'). Like the later 'Better Pot Luck' poster (see page 40) it works by putting the poster's message onto an everyday item – in this case frosted windows – and hoping that whenever viewers saw that same item in real life, they would be reminded of the poster's message.

◄ Eavesdropping Hitlers crowd around a British telephone box. This is one of a series of posters by a famous *Punch* cartoonist, Kenneth Bird (who called himself Fougasse). Many of his posters work by inserting Hitler into an everyday British scene, giving the impression that nowhere was safe from enemy ears.

► Abram Games illustrates the link between careless talk and the needless death of soldiers. The fact that they are stabbed in the back heightens the sense of betrayal.

YOUR TALK
MAY KILL YOUR COMRADES

A. GAMES.

PRINTED FOR H.M. STATIONERY OFFICE BY JAMES UPTON LTD., BIRMINGHAM & LONDON.   51—4059   P.R. No. 53

Women join up!

In the run up to war, the government started to encourage women to join the auxiliary forces. In 1938, the Auxiliary Territorial Service (ATS) and the Women's Auxiliary Air Force (WAAF) were set up. In 1939, the Women's Royal Naval Service (WRNS) was also formed. These services trained women for support roles in the armed forces to free men for the combat duties that women were not allowed to do. Women in the auxiliary forces worked as drivers, telephonists, engineers and clerks, amongst other jobs.

► 'The Blonde Bombshell' poster by Abram Games was designed to improve the dowdy image of the ATS. It was withdrawn, however, for making the ATS seem too glamorous (see page 47 for Games' second and final attempts).

JOIN THE ATS

ASK FOR INFORMATION AT THE NEAREST EMPLOYMENT EXCHANGE OR AT ANY ARMY OR A.T.S. RECRUITING CENTRE

◀ Despite their massive contribution, women were often valued not for the work that they did, but for freeing a man for active service. This poster was designed anonymously, but has a very similar style to the other recruitment posters by Abram Games.

What sort of women enlisted?

All types had turned up at Hallam Street to enlist – short, thin, small, dowdy, glamorous, typists and shop girls, married and single, from all walks of life.

Elsie Bartlett

▶ In another recruitment poster by Abram Games, the three planes flying over the recruit's right shoulder and the low perspective of the viewer make the WAAF woman seem strong and powerful.

Home forces

From 7 September 1940 until 16 May 1941 came the Blitz, when the Luftwaffe bombed London every night, except three. From September 1940 to May 1941, 50,000 high-explosive bombs were dropped on the capital. There was a serious threat of German invasion, so the government founded the Local Defence Volunteers (later called the Home Guard) in order to protect the British coastline and act as an early warning system, in case the Germans landed.

▶ These posters were aimed at men who were over the conscription age limit. Although the German invasion never happened, men like this often played a part in capturing German airmen who had been shot down over Britain.

The Germans are coming!

At the time of the fall of France there was a good deal of British joking going on – 'If they come here we'll do this and that' – and people were making the most comic preparations. My mother reckoned she'd be able to keep them off with a huge log fork. There was a patriotic woman in the village who never went about in her car without a row of pepper pots on the front. She thought she could blind the Germans when they arrived.

Myrtle Solomon

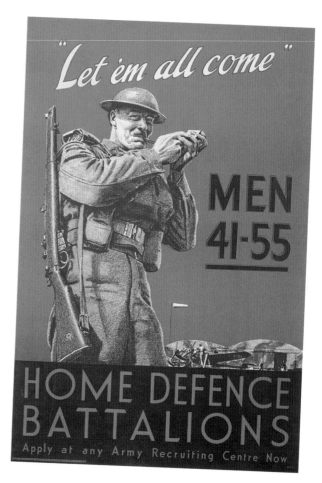

The AFS (see opposite) saves St Paul's Cathedral

There was a short sharp message from Winston Churchill to the fire services in London... saying that St. Paul's was to be saved at all costs... Every fireman knew without being told the target was St. Paul's... and without telling anyone they almost lined their backs up to St. Paul's and pointed their jets outwards to make sure no fire would reach St. Paul's... there was slight damage, but it was not destroyed – and yet the whole area around there was devastated.

Frederick Delve

▲ The AFS was formed in 1938 as part of the Air Raid Precautions. The London Fire Brigade was called out to 10,000 fires in the first 22 days of the Blitz alone.

Women at work

Women were desperately needed to do jobs on the land, in factories and elsewhere, which had previously been done by men. Posters portrayed these jobs as fun, exciting, noble and even heroic, and they inspired many women to start working between 1939 and 1941. However, insufficient volunteers forced the government to introduce compulsory registration of all women for employment in 1941. This was soon followed by the conscription of women to the uniformed auxiliary services. By June 1944, more than 7 million out of a total of 16 million women aged between 14 and 59, had been mobilised.

► The female factory worker pictured in this poster by Philip Zec looks almost as though she has released the aeroplanes out of her sleeves like a magician. Her smile, clothes and posture convey a mixture of power and ease not often found in earlier portrayals of women. The war dramatically changed attitudes towards women and their role.

WOMEN OF BRITAIN

COME INTO THE FACTORIES

ASK AT ANY EMPLOYMENT EXCHANGE FOR ADVICE AND FULL DETAILS

Women! You are needed in

THE NATIONAL
FIRE SERVICE
AS FULL-TIME OR PART-TIME MEMBERS

You can train to be a telephonist, despatch rider, driver, canteen worker and for many other duties.

APPLY FOR PARTICULARS TO NEAREST FIRE STATION OR EMPLOYMENT EXCHANGE

Printed for H.M. Stationery Office by Geo. Gibbons Ltd.   51-2219

▲ The detached head on this poster looks like a stone bust, conveying a nobleness further emphasised by the upwards, sideways angle of the gaze.

Keep going!

France, Belgium, the Netherlands and Luxembourg were invaded by the Germans on 10 May 1940. Neville Chamberlain resigned as Prime Minister and Winston Churchill took over. Britain – now facing the possibility of invasion herself – was in need of strong leadership.

▲ Posters used Churchill and his speeches as one way of inspiring the British and giving them a sense of common purpose.

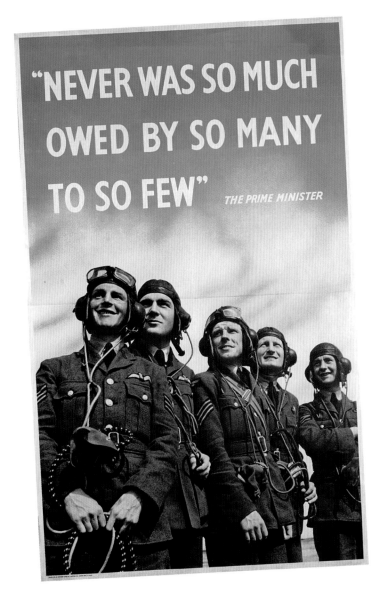

Business as usual!

Coming back to my house, those all around were bomb-blasted, and I saw this woman cleaning the front door of her demolished house as if it were business as usual! Often when a place was bombed in the East End, the King and Queen would come and visit. It would give the people a certain amount of heart. In fact, if we knew that they had a hit, it made us feel better, because it brought them down to our level. Yes, they did inspire people in their own way.

Doris Scott

◄ The quotation on this poster is abridged from Churchill's famous Battle of Britain speech, in which he said, 'Never in the field of human conflict was so much owed by so many to so few.'

These two posters were part of the 'Your Britain' series issued by the Army Bureau of Current Affairs in 1942. They featured images of Britain's past, present and future that the nation was fighting so hard to save.

◀ Designed by Frank Newbould, this poster shows an idyllic view of the South Downs. The style is similar to inter-war tourism posters that had encouraged people to travel by rail to the English countryside.

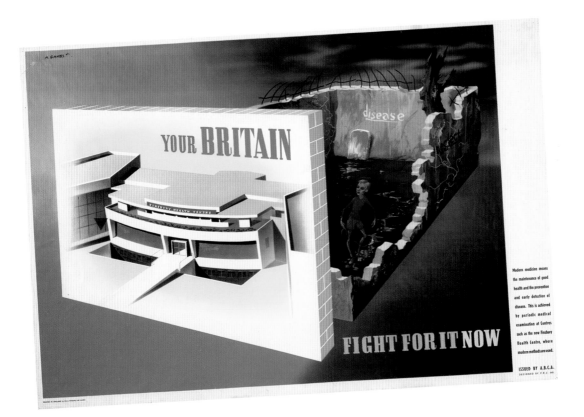

▲ Designed by Abram Games, this poster shows a vision of a better, more modern, future built on the ruins of war-damaged buildings. Intended to raise morale, the design was banned by Churchill, who thought that the image of a sickly child and a bombed-out building would adversely affect the troops' morale.

Britain's allies

Posters about Britain and her allies were often morale boosters, showing that the British were not alone and were fighting on the side of the good. They were also used to raise support for the new alliance between Britain and Russia after the latter were invaded by Hitler in June 1941. From July 1941 the Russians wanted Britain to open up a second front against Germany and stretch her resources.

◀ Determined-looking soldiers from Canada, Britain, New Zealand, Australia, West Africa, South Africa and India march shoulder to shoulder under the Union flag.

▼ This poster may seem purely informational, but it has an underlying message about the strength, size and importance of the British Empire.

All together now

The end of the war took away the purpose that for years had united young men of a dozen different countries in friendship and mutual loyalty, flying together and fighting together. It had been a way of life that few would ever experience again, even if for many it had been a way of death.

Frank Ziegler

▼ This poster ignores the differences between Britain and Soviet Russia and focuses on the common enemy, the Nazis.

SOVIET WAR POSTER

ДВЕ КРЕПКИЕ, КАК СТАЛЬ, РУКИ
ДРУГ К ДРУГУ БРАТСКИ МЫ ПРОСТЕРЛИ.
ОНИ, ВРАГА ЗАЖАВ В ТИСКИ,
СОМКНУТСЯ НА ФАШИСТСКОМ ГОРЛЕ!

TRANSLATION

TWO HANDS IN FRIENDSHIP, STRONG AS STEEL,
ONE TO THE OTHER ARE EXTENDED.
THE FASCIST THROAT THEIR GRIP WILL FEEL
THROTTLING TILL LIFE IS ENDED.

Rush British arms to RUSSIAN hands

A poster competition!

There was a schools' competition to make a poster about helping Russia with supplies to fight Hitler. John Perryn School sent mine in. It was of a giant British workman in overalls standing on a small coastline waving to a giant Russian soldier on a coastline who is waving back. Between them are long lines of little ships carrying boxes, guns, tanks and planes. I won a prize!

Brian Books

Waste not, want not

As part of the push to reduce reliance on imports, a number of posters tried to make the unglamorous habit of economising seem both fun as well as crucial to the war effort. Cartoons, like these of Hitler, Churchill and Mrs Sew-and-Sew, encouraged people to reduce consumption and reuse materials wherever possible. The Squanderbug made people feel guilty about spending spare money on anything other than war bonds.

◀ The choice between cooking up a pot of leftovers and baking a new pie is made into a matter of choosing sides in the war between Churchill and Hitler. By putting cartoons of the two leaders on a pot and pan, the designers hoped that people would be reminded of the poster when they used these everyday items.

◄ Clothing rationing came into effect on 1 June 1941. It became hard work to keep a family looking smart using clothing coupons. Mrs Sew-and-Sew was used as a role model to encourage women to improvise and remain positive. Details of local events could be written in the empty panel.

Clothing coupons

To accommodate my ever growing need for a large size shoe, everyone else in the family had to give up their coupons. We recycled clothes, which were cut down from adult clothes into something for children. We unpicked hand knitted jumpers, skeined and washed the wool and reknitted. Nothing was wasted.

Mrs D Edwards

► The Squanderbug, an image introduced by the National Savings Committee in January 1943, was widely found both in newspapers and on posters. It reminded people that spending money on luxuries was detrimental to the war effort.

Salvage!

As well as being told to reduce consumption and reuse things, people were asked to salvage things for recycling. Posters drew a link between domestic chores and winning the war. They appealed to women and children, who served the home front, by using an engaging style with cartoons, caricatures and puns to get their message across.

▶ This poster features a humorous and surreal image of worn-out clothes marching along without a body to fill them. Alongside, a dustman – proudly wearing First World War medal ribbons – gives his thumbs-up approval.

Battleships!

Things were of course in short supply at this time and an uncle hit on the idea of making toys out of wood and selling them to Busby's on Manningham Lane...Our dad took up his brother's idea and began to make large wooden battleships... there was a standing joke in our house with us imitating Dad's cry of, "Anyone want to buy a battleship?".

Dorothy Taylor

◀ Hitler is brought into the domestic setting to emphasise the importance of the new habits (such as recycling) that the government was promoting.

▶ This poster uses a cartoon-style picture of pigs in order to humanise them for the intended audience of mothers and children. Many people joined pig clubs, collecting kitchen waste to feed to pigs intended for slaughter.

Greedy pigs

We shared with a neighbour in the slaughter of a pig from time to time; we had to obtain a licence and forfeit part of our meat ration, although I doubt we ever did! Some we ate fresh, some was salted and the legs were smoked. Mr Bailey, the butcher, made lovely meaty sausages for us too... We had plenty of home-grown fruit and vegetables, but no oranges or bananas.

Mrs D Edwards

The end of Hitler

By the end of 1944, the Germans had been pushed back out of Russia by the Red Army and the Allies were advancing on Germany from the West. Hitler's reign finally came to an end when he killed himself in Berlin on 30 April 1945. What had started in 1933 with the promise of a glorious new age for Germany had ended ignominiously in defeat.

► This poster from 1932 is typical of the sort of image used to promote Hitler to the German population. The text suggests that the Nazis (National Socialists) can restore the greatness of Germany if everyone remains faithful and united.

► The poster opposite was a Russian design adapted by the British in 1941 when it was given to them by Stalin.

MANEATER

France
Greece
Jugoslavia
Rumania
Poland
Belgium

Printed in England by Stafford & Co., Ltd., Netherfield, Nottingham. 51-2231

Final words

On 7 May 1945, General Alfred Jödl signed an unconditional surrender on behalf of Grand Admiral Dönitz and the German people. On 8 May, Britain officially celebrated VE (Victory in Europe) Day. Churchill announced victory in a broadcast from 10 Downing Street. During a speech on the balcony of the Ministry of Health building on Whitehall he said to the crowd, 'This is your victory,' and the crowd spontaneously roared back, 'No – it's your victory!' A few days later, Churchill called a general election for July that year.

Churchill announces victory

God bless you all. This is your victory! It is the victory of the cause of freedom in every land. In all our long history we have never seen a greater day than this. Everyone, man or woman, has done their best. Everyone has tried. Neither the long years nor the dangers, nor the fierce attacks of the enemy, have in any way weakened the independent resolve of the British nation. God bless you all.

Winston Churchill

A different view of the war

I think that in Britain, the black market had undermined people's honesty, and I think as a society we were much less honest afterwards. I think it all started because we did scrounge petrol and nylons, and extra butter and so on. I think it all started in the war.

Margaret Gore

When the country voted, they voted for change and for the socialism that Churchill had warned against. The Labour Party won a landslide victory, giving it a majority of 146 seats in the Houses of Parliament. The effects of war were far from over. Rationing continued into the 1950s and Britain only finished paying off US and Canadian reconstruction loans at the end of 2006.

Some of the artists

Alfred Leete

Alfred Leete (1882-1933) started work as a printer, aged fifteen, before deciding to become a full-time illustrator when *Punch* magazine accepted one of his drawings in 1905. His Lord Kitchener design is probably the most famous of the First World War. It first appeared in September 1914 on the cover of the weekly magazine *London Opinion*.

Fougasse

Fougasse was the name used by the *Punch* cartoonist (Cyril) Kenneth Bird (1887-1965). It was a reference to a type of mine – possibly the type that injured him in the Gallipoli campaign in the First World War. In 1916 he made his first contribution to *Punch* as a cartoonist, and later became art editor and finally editor. He worked for the Ministry of Information during the Second World War and designed a number of posters for the 'Careless Talk Costs Lives' campaign.

Abram Games

Abram Games (1914-1996) was a superb designer who produced over 100 poster designs for the War Office between 1941 and 1946. He believed that, as the artist, he should be involved with the text on all of his posters and he wrote, 'I felt strongly that the high purpose of the wartime posters was mainly responsible for their excellence.'

▲ These three posters show Games' designs for the ATS recruitment brief. The first was banned for being too sexy, the second was rejected for looking too Soviet and the third was accepted as a perfect 'English rose'.

Frank Newbould

Frank Newbould (1887-1951) studied at Bradford College of Art and worked making designs for the RAF and the railways after the First World War. Early in the Second World War, Newbould designed the AFS poster (page 33) and was invited to join the War Office where he worked under Abram Games for the remainder of the war. His work was high-contrast, bright and positive, usually lacking the dark side that gave Games' work its edge and occasionally got it banned.

Glossary

Allies Britain and its Empire, the USA, USSR, France and China, which opposed the Axis Powers – Germany, Italy, Japan and others, in the Second World War. Sometimes used to refer to the 'Triple Entente'– Britain, France and Russia during the First World War.

armistice The laying down of arms in a war, which may or may not lead to a permanent peace agreement. Often refers to the First World War Armistice of 11 November, 1918.

Battle of Britain The attempt in 1940 by the German air force to defeat the Royal Air Force before a planned invasion of Britain by air and sea.

blackout A government-organised scheme to reduce lighting at night time in order to make it harder for enemy bombers to find their targets.

Blitz The bombing of British cities, and in particular London, by Germany from 7 September 1940 to 16 May 1941.

conscription A law requiring that all male citizens of a certain age serve in the armed forces as 'conscripts'.

conscientious objector Someone who refuses to be conscripted for moral or religious reasons.

enlistment The process of voluntarily joining the armed forces.

evacuation The removal in the UK of many women and most children from cities to the countryside where it was thought that they would be safe from German bombers at the outbreak of the Second World War.

Home Defence Battalions Groups formed during the Second World War of British men aged 41-55, who were ineligible for conscription, but were expected to help defend the country in the case of a German invasion.

hyper-inflation When inflation spirals out of control and the currency of a country loses its value.

John Bull A personification of Great Britain first created in 1712 by Dr John Arbuthnot. A fictional Englishman brought up on British beef and beer, he encapsulates the spirit of the island nation.

khaki From the Urdu word for dust (*khak*), khaki is a fabric or the colour of such fabric.

Luftwaffe The German air force.

merchant ships Any ships carrying tradable cargo from one port to another (as opposed to naval warships).

total war A war in which the entire nation and its economy are mobilised to defeat the enemy.

U-boat A German submarine (from the German word 'Unterseeboot' meaning 'undersea boat').

Western Front The contested armed frontiers between lands controlled by Germany to the East and the Allies to the West during the First World War.

Index